Mind Rustles

OrangeBooks Publication

Smriti Nagar, Bhilai, Chhattisgarh - 490020

Website: **www.orangebooks.in**

First Edition, 2023

Mind Rustles

SUBTLE THREADS OF SYLLABLES

DR UPMA A. SHARMA

OrangeBooks Publication
www.orangebooks.in

This book is dedicated to

*My beautiful family, soulful friends, colleagues and all
lovely readers.*

*I am grateful to everyone for having faith in me and for
constant motivation that never let me put the pen down.*

About the Author

Dr. Upma Aggarwal Sharma is a doctor by profession and heads the Community healthcare programme of India's leading Pharmaceutical Company under CSR. She studied MBBS from Govt. Medical College Patiala and Post-graduation in Health and family welfare management from National Institute of Health and family welfare, New Delhi.

Poetry is her passion and she has been writing for the last four decades. She feels that penning is the best way to satiate the appetite for words, words born out of ethos and notions, streaming their way out to ink.

About the book

This poetry book is an anthology of 55 poems that were borne out of mind rustles. Unsaid words immersed in ink having found their way onto the paper.

Readers shall be able to relate to most of the poems and feel the subtlety of sentiments.

All beautiful sketches have been drawn by my sweet little niece Devishi Gupta aka Chinu (my cousin Shefali's daughter). She is very creative and has an awesome hand in drawing. She keeps watching different sketching sites on YouTube and draws her inspiration from many budding artists.

Index

1. Memory lane

As I walk down the memory lane,

Plateaus of emotions whine and wane,

Grace on face stays

while smile deepens,

And wrinkles sprinkle

the essence of pretence in time.

2. Life is what you make it

Birth, the inception of life,

Reason to celebrate

joyous moments,

Taking great pride,

Body the chariot,

Soul passenger,

Mind is the one

that drives,

Check your thoughts,

Cultivate ideas,

Work hard,

Not for reward,

Your deeds decide,

The nascence of life,

Life is what

you make it,

Selfish or kind,

A humble mind,

Poor or rich,

Honest or witch,

Remember you must,

Shed everlasting lust,

Equality for all,

Do your very best,

Sooner or later,

All make peace,

Nothing will count,

Unannounced comes the death.

3. Your kiss from heavens

A little angel in my lap as I regained consciousness,

And the kiss came upon from heavens.

A bundle of joy in my hands,

And the bliss came upon from heavens.

A beaming smile and glitter in his eyes,

And our world glorified from heavens.

A father's love knew no bounds,

And subtle emotions came from heavens.

Abundant dreams that treasured the heart,

And endless longings solaced to heavens.

4. Setting of a dawn

orange twilight hues

of a beautiful sunrise ~

take to a clear sky

5. You are a super hero

Affectionate, witty and brilliant,

Joys and humour much rampant,

Muscular and macho for the bad,

You are a superhero, my dear dad!

Deeply disguised one day as I sat,

You read my face and gave me a pat,

Courage to beat the rogues at the pool,

Else I would have been proved a fool,

Remember the day at school I excelled,

You were teary-eyed, with joy so dwelled,

Never to forget your hugs and embrace,

Sparkle in your eyes and heavenly grace,

Days of picnics, fun and frolic are alive,

Swimming at resort and that deep dive,

Rock climbing and the river rafting,

Hospital bed and the bone grafting,

Taught me that life is a lemonade,

World is worth living with truth and traits,

Help the needy; believe in hard work, not fate,

You are a superhero, dad; you are truly great!

6. Revelation

Any gentle knock...

and I get up so spontaneously,

No tangible grounds for suspicion,

still, I would patronise.

And settle down later in despair.

My eyes rest still on portal...

as he longs for a revelation,

Unshakable to his intrigue,

mind undergoes fixation.

And I sit in my seat where I am.

Leaving my thoughts free to navigate...

7. Subtle threads of syllables

Threads of

Infinite length,

Subtle and colourful,

Getting entwined;

Rainbow,

Brilliant colours,

As threads of rain lengthen,

Blissful delight;

Vibrant

Hues of passion,

Set heartstrings into rhythm,

Sweet song in the air!

8. Amazing artist

The most original and the perfect one,

A magnetic force, every moment attracts,

My ultra-favourite since day one,

Nothing, be it living or non-living, ever distracts,

Amazing artist GOD, at will, adds or subtracts!

9. Vacation humour

Our sponsor papers much earlier had reached,

To my dear sister, we had promised,

This vacation we were to spend in Brisbane,

Surgeon declared an emergency, plans in vain,

Oh, a trip to Australia landed up in the hospital instead!

Planned a gala party at home,

Leaving unturned not a single stone,

Invitation sent to esteemed guests,

The sickness left me quite stressed,

Food bland soups, no lavish bone!

Planned to meet beloved on a bright day,

Dressed in my favourite blue, I was on my way,

Much to my agony, he said he was stuck,

A bad vacation it was, and my bad luck,

Consoled myself, thinking he must be gay!

10. Chasing Rainbow

Eyes

staring

constantly

at the closed door;

For years waiting to see him return home.

11. *Songs of power*

Dreaming of vivid colours

yet painting in black,

Singing vibrancy of life

still living in the dark,

Cherishing freshness in the air

yet feeling suffocated,

As if conscious veiled by

fumes of depression...

No sunshine reaches

as murky clouds blanket,

All greens and oranges

appear grey in Ishihara,

When the train of thoughts

rams into the unkind,

Just to leave collecting

chips of memories...

The palette smears all its colours,

Brushes the veins as red cries,

And tears stain the cheeks black,

Soul engulfed into the smoke of eternity...

12. *Summer solstice*

As Sun appeared to stand still in the sky,

Hence the Latin term solstice arised,

Summer sweltered till to fierce heat's wilt,

Came closer to Sun, earth with elliptic tilt,

Be it reason for season's conquest,

Summer solstice brought renewal and good harvest,

Fascination marked by the Stonehenge,

And Ireland's prehistoric Newgrange,

Guru Purnima, international surfing day or music day,

Washington celebrates Fremont solstice parade,

Arctic Circle sees the Sun on horizon at midnight,

As places north see Sun 24 hours shining bright.

13.   *Trust my love*
Anacreontic verse

Your sweet thoughts,

Heartbeats missed,

My passion

still put to the tests,

Feelings of love

why should I prove?

Swear by God

and tell lies,

Jump from height,

Feign into waters,

Cut the arteries,

Show the blood flow,

Will that mean?

See me simmer

slowly inside,

As distrust shouts

and nibbles my soul,

Challenge my patience

to eyes' constant stare,

Dried-up tears

and streaked cheeks,

Not a life moves,

I am better dead.

14. *Mystic Vision*

Until the inner sonorous cues

reverberate to make believe the surreal,

As murmurous truth

walks down the corridors,

Once again, to rest arcane,

To be unfolded...

While its gorgeous radiance

dazzling white amidst darkness,

Makes all black evanesce,

Unveils the thaumaturgic clouds,

To a soulful vision...

15. *Waiting – what's next*

An anxiety of a wait...

As I anticipate

sunrise each morning,

A pleasant day ahead

beguiles the mood,

Swift train of thoughts

brings smile on the face,

Fleet of birds

that aim sky high,

Moments that chirp

and dreams full of life,

A never-ending wait,

what must be next?

Many hearts beat

as red glows on cheeks,

No mind is waiting

for disasters to happen,

I cherish the present

till gates of heavens open.

16. *Castles*

Medieval towns, the citadels,

As fortified large ornate fascinate,

Engulfed my flaming true passion

that still echoes inside huge walls,

Sound of glittering brave swords

that took to cowardly deceit,

Condemned moonlight

as we met used to greet,

Midnight shadows over walls of castles

now are lost in a ghostly fleet,

Like a horrid dream

that makes my heart bleed,

Castles are a history

as lingers my life in a plead,

Silky pearl white gown stained in red,

Clouds of long hair left to shred,

Emotionless eyes that only stare,

Cruel men in hues of red painted scare,

In the name of honor for the race,

My true love was called a disgrace,

Corpses these dominating walls could capture

as souls serene, floated in enrapture,

In the era of humanity, I wish to be born again,

When race, colour and religion castles will be slain!

That place, these secrets,

Harbors more than a majestic face,

Captive, breath-taking enchanted beams,

Silver light waits down each hallway,

The eyes of men -prey- preyed on castle walls,

Vengeance broke the silence

as true love was met by fate

under a bleeding lune.

Loud wails come from despair,

Dragon statues look up to the flames,

Passion perfectly preserved!

Blood feuds between villages,

Tunics distinguished by color

Selfish toxins in the bloodstream,

Confession of the sins,

Green eyes full of dreams,

Lanterns lead each path,

Every page is torn until no more,

Beauty ignored by the dark!

Gems of honor, heal each plea,

A love story paved with a wrench,

light twinkles, wisps through the rocks,

Beyond enchanted blocks,

Coat of Arms rises to guard these ground,

Love conquers all when united!

17.   *Instincts of innocence*

Chastity belt on,

The pretence of oblivion,

Is the current human mind

soaked deep in all wrongs,

Selfish and cruel;

As newborns cry naïveté,

Guiltless greens call

and pure flowing waterfall,

Rains pledge washing away

as the breeze swirls,

Butterflies flutter as

nectar drips on nature's platter;

O, man! With a guilty blush

clear on your face,

Can you defy those crimes,

Prove to be in nescience?

Reverberate your inner self,

That pure youthfulness

with which you were born,

The virtue of your charm,

Enlightened soul, a kind subtle heart,

Imbued deep still,

Is altruistic instinct of innocence?

18. A new species

Cunning cheating

and then fleeting,

Machiavellian many,

crafting and contriving,

Deceptive dishonest,

frankly defrauding,

Slaughtering slaying,

bloodshed of massacre,

Conflicts and combats,

enmity and warfare,

Uncaring unfriendly,

Barbarous and brutal,

Savage sadistic,

Cruel and unsympathetic,

Cold-hearted, cold-blooded,

Insensitive Inhumane.

Contrary to what

God had created,

Is it some new species?

19. *Joys of Spring*

An onset of early spring,

Benevolence floats in the air,

Colours full of romance,

Dancing greens to trance,

Eternal bliss!

Flowers bloom to enchant,

Golden millets of wheat,

Happiness will surely greet,

Iridescent bow in sky,

Jazzy kids jiggle,

Kites fly up so high,

Lovers craving for meets,

Meddle into the streets,

Natter and laugh out loud,

Oblivions the talk of the town,

Passion in heart grows,

Quaffs the sorrows,

Reminisce and reveal,

Salients of joy unveil,

Thrive to show zeal,

Unending positivity,

Vows to fill the air,

Wanderers waited out for,

Xenons at the night shout,

Yearnings ride a high horse,

Zephyr sets the perfect flair!!

20. *Brevette*

Heart

T h u m p s

Emotions.

Wrestler

P u n c h e s

Opponent.

Ink

P e n s

Words.

21. *Memories beyond time*

Once embracing my tender wrists,

now, tired watches lay dropped on woods,

Waking me up with the first ray of sun, asleep with set,

only to find years and decades pass by,

Constant Memories that keep me introspecting,

as I see the twilight appear and wither,

Proving Einstein's theory of relativity,

while people are lost in materialism,

I am being spendthrift with words so sublime,

anticipate they live even after the concluding day,

On every timeline hangs a malignant memory,

to create history and for moving on and on!!

22. *Give me no limits*

Limitless sky

and vast ocean,

No boundaries

breaths will follow,

Sunshine pierces

the minutest,

Moon brushes in sleep,

God created no limits!

Why should I,

His daughter,

follow any limits, O' man,

That you created

just to subjugate?

What to wear,

When to laugh,

Whom to talk,

Making friends with,

Why these limits??

Putting a full stop

to my thoughts,

No freedom

of expression

or education,

Snatching rhythm

off my heartbeats,

Am I not human?

Unacceptable are;

The narrow visions

that don't let us grow,

Gender inequality

that ought to raise a brow,

Don't measure my span

as I take a flight,

Care for my emotions,

Give me no limits!

23.   *Spectacular*

Stunning sky had a thrilling effect,

Prominently painted by a dramatic sunset.

Elegant aura of dusk seen, on the horizon,

Could see fiery flames of passion wisen.

To a poet's pen and a mind's vision,

Anticipating the reader's thoughtful precision,

Creator with man was at His best array,

Unfolding intellect and imaginative display,

Last vows kept were like a subtle miracle,

Adding mettle to heart and face all debacles,

Remarkable viewing with nature's spectacle.

24. Sohni Mahiwal – Love epic

Love has ever retained its glow,

for years and centuries have passed,

True to its eternal constant flow,

in history, etched and cast.

When Sohni swam across in no boat,

as every evening craved her bare soul,

Held an earthen pot that kept her afloat,

as the sun slowly slid to the other pole,

Soul mate Mahiwal waited at the bank,

as she emerged from the water serene,

The world tagged them as crank,

an ocean as if walked to the supreme,

Lost in absolute zero, the two daily met,

till the envied dears played a foul game,

The trust woke up to a life's regret,

the punctured pot, waters were in flame,

Waves engulfed to set them free,

united by death, they rode the tides,

Heavenly abode beyond the skies,

Alive in hymns as their souls sing out!

25. Dumbstruck

Disguise, I find myself,

Deceit his vanity,

Diabolism doesn't work,

Devil can't cite scriptures?

Distress is camouflaged,

Doing only delight,

Dumbstruck, why should I be?

26. Tom and Jerry

A little creature would creep

and make Tom honestly weep,

Bright ideas the cat would design,

With a fail always, gears up to redefine,

We could sit through the whole night

and giggle over their silly fight,

Trying to catch the clever mouse

and win confidence of the lady of the house,

Tom would plan and lay the trap

as Jerry brilliantly discovers to unwrap,

She would fall into her own dug ditch

and witty mouse merrily sings at a pitch,

Year after year, still unable to resist,

These funny comics are at the top of my list!

27. When memories bind

tears embellish eyes

memories of childhood flash

I meet my brother…

28. Song of Life

You and me, me and you,

Every morning is sweet and new,

Love sublime and fresh as dew,

You and me, me and you,

You and me, me and you,

You and me, me and you,

Fortunate and blessed we are,

Precious our love, joy our life,

You and me, me and you,

You and me, me and you,

You and me, me and you,

Dreamers we are, yet living to full,

Not letting go and holding on still,

You and me, me and you,

You and me, me and you,

You and me, me and you,

Deeper the bond, the shorter the life,

No worries and no strife,

You and me, me and you,

You and me, me and you,

You and me, me and you,

All songs I wanted to sing,

Oh, the melody, you added a zing,

You and me, me and you,

You and me, me and you!

Oh, don't let go,

You and me,

Oh, don't let go,

You and me,

Just a little blow,

Me and you,

Just a little blow,

Me and you,

Live to your full,

Come, sing with me,

Live to your full,

Come, sing with me,

Life is a miracle,

God's greatest miracle!

29.   *The Good Newspaper*

A bright morning with lovely sunshine,

Garden of my house and the teatime,

Fingers going quickly in page flicker,

Eager to read the good newspaper.

A man putting a mask on an injured cat,

And the dog, full of affection gives a pat,

Compassion in the heart of mankind,

That for years had been mentioned blind.

We have conquered much with thoughts,

Could fly through skies and run on rails,

The good newspaper says we have won on crime,

No more thefts and killings cry of the time.

No rich, no poor; all blessed alike,

Every life He created with equal delight,

But in unison with all, we are living with leisure,

Nature at its best; what a pleasure!

No wars, no boundaries; an end to hatred,

Colour caste and creed, no more catered,

No Greed or envy, defy the basis of strife,

Living present to full the best rule of life!

30. Memories of good old days

When memories give you tears,

You sit; there is nowhere to go,

And you have the worst of fears,

Can you ever retain your glow?

Those nostalgic evening walks,

Drives in the dark that made crazy,

Stuck in mind like stubborn plaques,

Can those pictures ever go hazy?

Engraved in marble, you can't erase,

Successive thoughts bound to depress,

Echoing in ears stays every phrase,

Alive are memories you must confess,

Emotions flow with good old memories,

As souls dance serene in mind galleries!

31. *Holodomor Genocide*

Native of Ukraine and the Soviet Union,

Known once for my independence,

Was pitied to brutal artificial famine,

Exporting our grain and leaving us to die,

Declared Kurkul under Stalin's policy,

Shipped to remote uninhabited Siberia,

Left to die of famine,

I was one of the millions,

Once the landlords now riches to rags,

Ghost of hunger that engulfed us all,

Even our innocent kids,

Many nights of darkness and severe ache,

More in the heart than in the stomach,

Sun brought no shine,

Zero hope as death danced around,

As if wolves driven from the woods,

We ate our own bodies,

Every moment souls died a new death,

Horrible Helplessness, hue and cry around,

Walking amongst corpses,

The goods were first to die,

Cannibalism survived,

Could morals stay high?

Survival was a mystic miracle,

Made to deny any famine in public,

Robert's conquest termed it, 'Harvest of Sorrow',

Decree by Parliament proves it worst of genocide!

**On Holodomor in Ukraine in 1928*

32.   *Past lives*

Incarnation and a better life,

Has always been a human strife,

Strange curiosity to excavate,

Living cool present, yet divagate,

Since age of three, I yearned to fly,

Little sweet cuckoo I always spied,

Melody of voice I could imitate,

As an echo, I could reciprocate,

Birth of life, dying getting revived,

A closer look to the soul came much alive,

I declared dead as life belied,

Watched dear ones in deep disguise,

Made me introspect; what's horoscope?

A friend took me to a teller's grove,

He then showed me the leaves of Bhrigu Samhita,

Three consecutive births on the leaf of my chakra,

Mine and my parents' names to my surprise,

Centuries before, how could he ever write,

All were true, as if just for me to apprise,

Unbelievable a cuckoo in the past; am I wise?

Bygone are the precious past lives,

No bees, no honey, just empty hives,

History, sometimes the best teacher,

Can evolve into a top preacher!

Based on real personal happening.

** Maharishi Bhrigu in Treta yuga during the Vedic period prepared a unique astrological horoscope where every human, born at any point of time - past, present or future can find his chakra according to date, time, and place of birth.*

And a collection of his leaves is known as Samhita (Hindi word means collection)

So Bhrigu Samhita has all of us with our past and future lives!

And of course, a present too, in fact, it starts with the present!

33. Tidal locking

Like waxing and waning

of the moon, his love shuddered,

The tidal locking

that hampered my zing,

Effulgent life lost

on darker side of the silvery moon.

In its brightness

drowned my shimmer,

Then it abated into a sickle

to slice my pride,

Forlorn, I chose to live by

the dark side of the moon.

Consumed by its force,

deep on this side of the earth

where peace calls my name,

I lean and stay,

over the reflection of waves

on the dark side of the moon.

The horizon rips my heart,

two bodies weaken

by its physical use

and tidal locking,

Welcoming and affecting everything

on the dark side of the moon.

Tidal locking- Tidal forces from Earth slow down the
rotation of the moon, and the same side faces the Earth.
The other side, the darker side always remains dark.

34. *In the library*

Beyond the world

our meeting place,

Where studious read

we met in grace,

All those days

and years of togetherness…

In my college library…

Remember the day

when the librarian noticed,

As we sat beside

no words spoken,

No books issued,

neither in our hands…

The library, we were shown the door…

Shared our notes

and thence the thoughts,

Polished were we

glittered the wroughts,

Learnings of life

those degrees defied...

In the library to our soul...

My second home

ever since he left,

Lit desire of knowing

the logic of my being alive,

As I dug deeper

knowledge wiped my tears,

Those crispy leaves

of books in the library...

Familiar shelves

still await my touch,

As the leaves I unfold

and lend my emotions,

To be the novels

that have read high,

For all times to come...

In my college library...

35. *You make me exist*

butterflies flutter

petals take vibrant colors

honey in beehive...

orange of twilight

reflects into the ocean

beautiful sunrise...

a magnetic charm

gentle breeze touches the soul

as birds fly afloat...

nature sings in grace

earth meets sky at horizon

existence proven...

not a word from you

as eyes stare at the blue

I cease to exist...

passionate longing

rhythmic drumming beats say

you are my sole heart...

36. *Agony of an Unborn*

The safest in world was a mother's womb,

An affection flowed into my veins,

Until they turned it into my tomb,

Who can imagine those creeping pains,

Innocent life taken before inception,

Was this to meet anybody's gains?

Unaware of those webs of deception,

Showed myself up with great cheers,

Thousands nurtured, why me an exception?

My genitors, who were the most dears,

Turned out to be my ruthless killers,

Stabbing and piercing me with spears,

My tale may not figure amongst chillers,

Veiled story probably never will unfold,

Else could have been the best of thrillers,

Not a word, vanishing even before being told,

Where I was being shaped into pure gold,

The safest in world was a mother's womb,

Until they turned it into my tomb!

37. An Autumn Intermingled

When twilight sends lavender to the sky,

And reflections of light ignite the orange,

(Alluring colours of autumn mesmerise),

Sickle of moon is unable to cut the dark,

(Unfathomed beauty in orange and yellow),

Robust waters of rivers to shores' embark,

(Trenchant evanescence of greens),

Crispy leaves with breeze flutter around,

(Unfeigned emotions true up in zest),

Yellow, orange and red hues surround,

(Mollify the fiery torrid days),

An autumn night awaits a warm welcome,

(Nautical furnaces red on edge of horizon)!

38. Heaven on earth

End to wars, enmity and strife,

A heaven on earth it will be,

Utmost value, respect for life,

Hearts beating in love and all glee,

Above self and prejudiced we,

Flowers will bloom be it autumn,

Faith and belief in full quantum,

Content and peace will find their way,

Fragrance of hope spreads, dreams blossom,

Heaven will walk on earth that day!!

39. *A Dad's daughter*

An exquisite and true copy of my soul,

I see my tomorrow in her.

Bliss from the heavens, she entered my life,

Really is the sparkle of my eyes.

Brought up with extreme delicacy and subtlety,

She is the best thing that ever happened to me.

A bundle of joy so affectionate,

Makes me forget the day's weary jade.

Greets with a smile that rejuvenates,

Bubbling with emotions ever and always.

Sweeter to a bee's envy,

An angel with a magic wand.

My prized possession, she's precious to me,

Never shall we part; she is unsliverable of me!!

(A dad's feelings for his

Daughter)

40. *Remembering when*

I remember when…

We would climb up the trees in peak sun,

And scared of the gardener though,

Yet pluck fruits and just have fun,

And he could never catch us…

I remember when…

We would sit on benches in the college cricket ground,

And cheer up our classmates for a win,

Yet making loud whistling sounds,

And in disguise, the opponents would run…

I remember when…

I saw my life-mate for the first time,

And flattened in love at first sight,

Yet craving for the joys abound,

And woke up each day with a new sky…

I remember when…

He took me on a long drive,

And I found ethereal delight as he kissed my soul,

Yet I reached the end of the earth,

And consummate desires pacified…

41. *Above the clouds*

When I gazed at the sky,

Was devoid of celestial bliss to the eye,

Pitch dark, as dark as a black lie.

Obscured 'above the clouds' were,

Moon of my emulations and stars of materialism,

Rising to the infinite expanse and unlimited realm.

Ambitions coursed like blood through me,

Material desires unending like treadmill,

Unseeable above murky dark clouds of philistinism.

Enthusiasm lost to adversities and fortune,

For lack of determination altered my traverse,

Time tricked me down like a running grave,

Rainbow that receded as I advanced.

As the wind blew and the doors rattled,

Saturated clouds burst with the torrential rain,

Sweeping impatience and increased appetite,

Cleared sky of ambitions as hollow as soul of an echo.

Iniquity flees, and I find,

My verve, as new as the glistening silk of the moon,

Determination as hard as a rock,

Metamorphosed into a millionaire's mistress.

And tireless I fly, conforming to all my aspirations,

Culminating at the crest, desires hurried like clouds,

And diligent I stand in complacency,

Where serenity is the denouement.

42. Whispers of light

Deep in distress, life could not be a better hell,

When needles of all clocks ceased to move,

All my virtues stranded, zero a perfect word,

Then I heard whispers of light!

Fast the clouds ran, came the sun so sublime,

Engulfed ghosts of gloom, spread jollity shine,

Deep wounds on my soul, healed ahead of time,

Here came my miracle man, and so the whispers of light!

Butterflies danced, and the flowers blossomed,

The enchanting wind carried on broods of vigour,

Sowed into my heart to grow up with every beat,

I followed the whispers of light!

Hope is a good breakfast but a bad supper,

The air hung heavy after the storm, brooding,

Time is like a snake that swallows its own tail,

Groom in time, Esoteric are the whispers of light!!

43. The umbrella

Two travellers unknown

Never having met

Different roads taken

Hear dissimilar drummers,

The meeting is predestined

Share their ideology

Come closer as their

Heartbeats rhyme,

Together get along

Side by side

On the same road

Under one umbrella,

Colorful surrounds bloom

Nature follows them

Cherish togetherness

Under The Same Umbrella!!

44. Dedication

Perseverance of the intense bees

and iron-will of the frisky spider,

Tiny self-disciplined ants queue up,

ascend cliffs in an endeavour,

Subtle Moth embraces flame

while robust wins the muscle game;

Passion at borders sets ablaze,

high heaps of enemies at the gate,

Dedicated heroes of war return

as twenty-one cannons decorate.

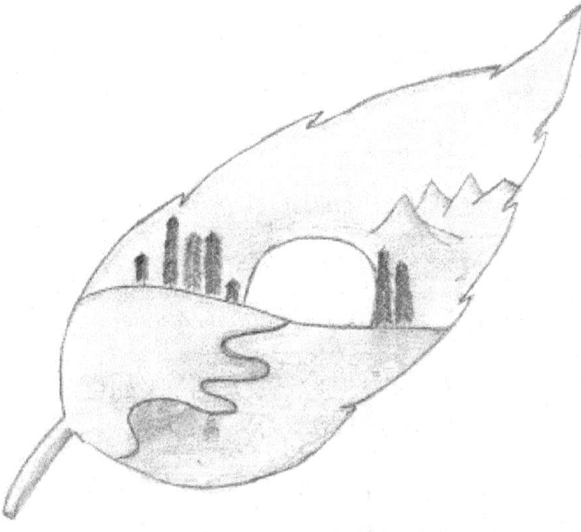

45.   *Here comes the sun*

Yellow rays reflect golden

sparkle into air,

Glitter into eyes; heat that we

yearned, soothes,

Here comes the sun!!

Frozen blood melts and

numbness flays,

Haziness in sky flees and

evenings lengthen,

Hibernation of all life is over!

Yellow mustard stands high in

fields,

Sunflower turns and vows head

to sun,

Each life reverberates sunshine!

Wintery winds are near to

conquer,

Radiant cheerfulness subdues

cold,

Here comes the sun!!

46. *Living in present*

Bygone is past, memories echo,

No one can live in antiquity,

There's no time like the present,

Future comes apace, an opaque mirror,

Live a life of endeavour, live to your full,

Till the air is able to fill!!

Achievements, the jewels of past,

The present is the very life of life,

Why ponder over the future, unknown pal,

Also, when it comes soon enough,

Live present moments in happiness,

Water that ought to flood!!

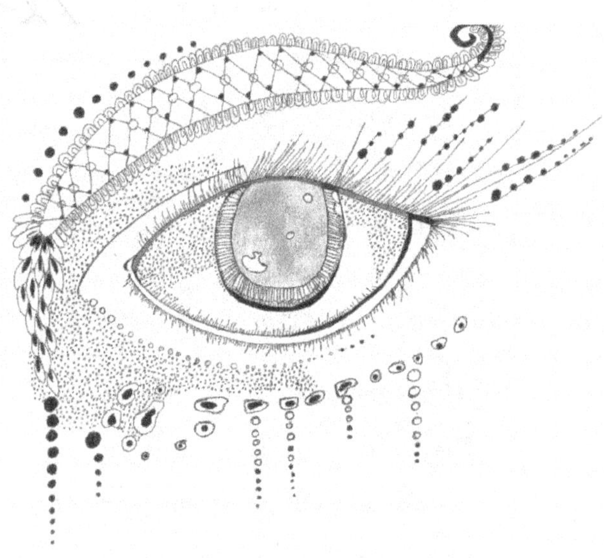

47. *Diamond in your eyes*

Strange are the ways of passion,

Rising in love with each meet,

My appetite goes more intense,

Can't I see Diamonds in your eyes!

An unending journey in a sandy desert,

Sun at its vertex and more and more thirst,

The sudden sight of water; be it a mirage,

Can't I see Diamonds in your eyes!

The gratification only with the best,

You will not settle for the common rest,

Glad, even if it's "A diamond's remnants",

Can't I see Diamonds in your eyes!

Your magnetic charm creates waves in my heart,

Don't pretend calm and keep me at bay,

You don't ever evince, nor do you state,

But can't I see Diamonds in your eyes!!

48. Santa Claus

Children scream with joy

on sight of chubby, plump,

white-bearded Santa,

In a red coat with

white collars and cuffs,

red trousers and fur cap.

With gifts in his bag

and a shaking belly,

He comes laughing,

Riding on a sleigh

driven by eight reindeers,

As Rudolph, the red-nosed,

drives through the night,

lands swiftly on roofs

and slides into houses through chimneys,

Chuckles, Ho! Ho! Ho!

and drops gifts for all,

A year's long wait ends

as wish list turns into reality,

Midnight hours...

Popping of firecrackers,

Church bells ring

and Carols sing,

Celebrating birth

of Jesus Christ,

It's Christmas time!!

Like a zephyr, he buzzes,

gifts to well-behaved

and guilty foraged,

And then visits markets,

streets, the whole city,

To return to his home

at the North Pole,

Collects request letters

and gifts throughout the year,

For the next Christmas!!

49. *Dear diary*

Stealthy romanticism,

Where else can hide,

Than my dear diary!

Twinkling of the eyes,

Time of one's life,

Enrapture!

Blush on a face,

Warmth of caress,

Ends the chase!

Whispers of heart,

Vibes of mystique,

And final embrace!

Moments captivated,
Clicked in no time,
Penned into verse!

No poem means,
Yet muster in
And inscribe!

Take it inside you,
O my dear diary,
Else memories fade!

Draft so peppery,
Seeks desperate hideout
Rests Everlasting Eternal!

50. *Imagination*

Power of fancy,

Over good reason,

My imagination!

A force of nature,

Trust or truth,

The delight of an immature?

No war, no red earth,

No remonstrance,

A fascination?

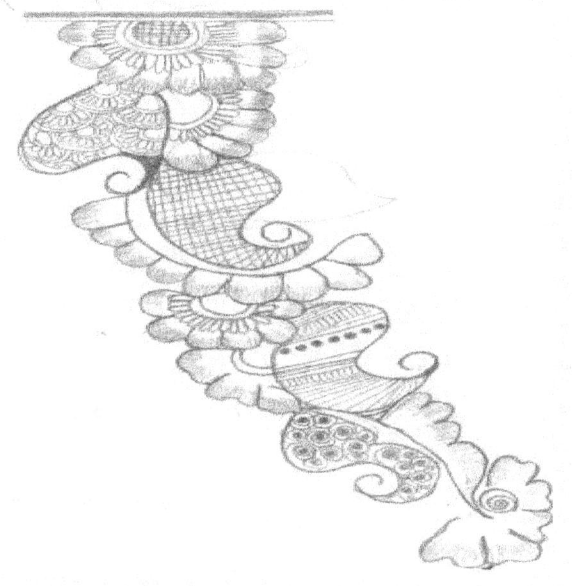

Bumptious or chagrined,

Deeply possessed neurotic,

An absconding notion?

Pulling me into a pool of love,

Then announce exile,

Inchoate insight?

My imagination,

Makes me a fool,

A weird hallucination?

51.   Beautiful

Best of His creation, we, the humans,

Endeavour to be kind to all life and nature,

Actually exploit its vibrant subtle being,

Unending mysteries of vast deep seas,

The nurturing soil and the refreshing air,

Immense beauty that eyes could perceive,

Follow through the universe and the Milky Way,

Unveil even in pitch dark as stars twinkle,

Lost in the aura of sun's twilight and moon's silver.

52. Into the blue

dark clouds evanesce

as eyes stare into the blue

ecstasy shimmers...

serene ocean depths

awaiting reconnaissance

undulate their throbs...

53.   *Girl rising*

Years of oppression and no revolt,

Continued suffering of subtle minds,

I don't find girl rising!

Living in a subjugation and cruel society,

Abused by her own beloved,

I don't see any girl rising!

The call for justice is far from a cry,

Targeting her from every side,

I don't find any girl rising!

Awakening minds is the only tool,

Raise a voice against despotism,

Inoculate courage into the oppressed,

Sun will appear above the horizon,

Ascent with an active rebellion,

I can definitely see the girl rising!!

54. A Conquest

When ink of romance

subdues respect for nature,

Exploitation begins,

Treasures seem perpetual,

Obliterated thoughts

drop down the curtains,

Devastation knocks

on constant failure to unveil,

A wake-up call; wake up,

With a hunger to introspect,

Satiate this appetite,

Howbeit, the fancy foods,

A conquest...

For luscious bequests

bestowed by Him,

Instead of drinking coffee

in cafes of Berlin.

55. *Victory over dark*

Awful darkness annoys

and withers in amazing glitter,

Gruesome grim on the face

turns delightful,

Frightened girls are fortunate

to be finding light,

Monoliths shine brighter in the moon

than in the museum,

Oval and opaque sculptures

opening ways to glory,

As their pride preludes

and black patronises,

Vicious cycle of

vindictive darkness ends,

Light of new morning

emerges Victorious!